OTHER BOOKS BY HELEN EXLEY:

Over 50s' Jokes

Over 70s' Jokes

Over 80s' Jokes

Golf Jokes

Giggles A joke book

Cat Jokes

365 Happy Days!

Life! And other disasters... 365

The Happiest Little Thoughts in the whole world

EDITED BY HELEN EXLEY

Published in 2019, 2022 by Helen Exley ®LONDON in Great Britain.
Design, selection and arrangement © Helen Exley Creative Ltd 2019, 2022.
All the words by Stuart & Linda Macfarlane, Stuart Macfarlane, Jayne King,
Linda Gibson, Bill Stott, Jenny de Souza, Helen Exley, Caley O'Rourke,
Brian Clyde, Charlotte Gray, Pam Brown, Nicole Reubens, Helen Thomson,
Amanda Bell, Mathilde Forestier, Paulette Caron copyright
© Helen Exley Creative Ltd 2019, 2022.
Cartoons copyright © Bill Stott 2019, 2022.
The moral rights of the authors have been asserted.

12 11 10 9 8 7 6 5 4 3 2 1

ISBN: 978-1-78485-234-4

Helen Exley ® LONDON,
16 Chalk Hill, Watford, Herts WD19 4BG, UK
www.helenexley.com

Over 60's Jokes

CARTOONS BY BILL STOTT

Helen Exley

If I had my life to live again, I'd make the same mistakes, only sooner.

TALLULAH BANKHEAD

Everything irritates me.
Everything annoys me.
Everything frustrates me.
It would appear that I have turned
into a Grumpy Old Git!

STUART & LINDA MACFARLANE

Finally I have found
a make-up that
completely hides wrinkles –
it's two parts sand
to one part cement.

JAYNE KING

Age : That period of life
in which we compound for the vices
that remain by reviling those ·
we have no longer the vigour
to commit.

AMBROSE BIERCE

Exercise daily, eat

wisely, die anyway.

AUTHOR UNKNOWN

A person of sixty
has spent twenty years in bed
and over three years eating.

ARNOLD BENNETT

Middle age:
When you are sitting
at home
on a Saturday night
and the telephone rings
and you hope
it isn't for you.

OGDEN NASH

An archaeologist
is the best husband
a woman can have;
the older she gets,
the more interested he is in her.

AGATHA CHRISTIE

There's many
a good tune
played on
an old fiddle.

SAMUEL BUTLER

Last night
my partner
and I
had a night
of wild,
unadulterated
passion –
we played Scrabble
until two
in the morning.

STUART & LINDA MACFARLANE

Sex got me into trouble from the age of fifteen: I'm hoping that by the time I'm seventy I'll straighten it out.

HAROLD ROBBINS

Old is... when you look in the mirror and think to yourself "Aren't I wise".

MARCELLA MARKHAM

I don't want to achieve immortality through my work. I want to achieve immortality through not dying.

WOODY ALLEN

REPORTER:
"What do you expect the future to be like?"
OLDER WOMAN:
"Very short."

AUTHOR UNKNOWN

Except for the occasional heart attack,
I feel as young as I ever did.

ROBERT BENCHLEY

At twenty we worry
about what others
think of us,
at forty we don't care
what they think of us,
and at sixty
we discover they haven't
been thinking of us at all.

BOB HOPE

BALDNESS:
THE FRINGE BENEFITS

1. There is never any hassle with dress codes, flaky dandruff or trying to get that full-bodied look.

2. You save countless hours and dollars at hair salons.

3. You can use your head as a reflector when lost at sea.

DAVID E BESWICK

I used to have a sign
over my computer that read:
OLD DOGS
CAN LEARN NEW TRICKS,
but lately I sometimes ask myself
how many more new tricks
I want to learn.
Wouldn't it be easier
just to be outdated?

BABA RAM DASS

Life is a moderately
good play with
a badly written third act.

TRUMAN CAPOTE

What's the good of having
something to look forward to,
if I can't remember what it was?

ASHLEIGH BRILLIANT

Sixty is the time to get up and go
before everything else does.

PAM BROWN

The older I get,

My Keep Young and Beautiful Mantra:
I am not getting old.
My face is not wrinkled like a rhino.
That twinge is definitely not rheumatism.
My knees work perfectly –
most of the time.
Ouch, ooh, eech, oh ah, ouch...

STUART & LINDA MACFARLANE

You know you're over sixty when you daren't stop on a busy high street in case some do-gooder wants to help you across the road.

MIKE KNOWLES

the older old is.

TOM BAKER

The man flattered himself
that he was still a ladies' man,
and decided to flirt with
the comely waitress.
"So tell me, Sweetheart,
where have you been all my life?"
he crooned.
"Actually, Sir," she pointed out sweetly,
"for the first forty-five years of it,
I wasn't even around."

AUTHOR UNKNOWN

The advantage of great age,
huge wealth and
complete ownership
is that you can say
anything you like,
you boring young idiot!

BILL STOTT

I must be getting
absent-minded.
Whenever I complain
that things aren't
what they used to be,
I always forget
to include myself.

GEORGE BURNS

How foolish to think
that one can ever slam the door
in the face of age.
Much wiser to be polite and gracious
and ask him to lunch in advance.

NOËL COWARD

A young real estate agent was pushing
hard to sell an apartment
to this old codger. After praising its
numerous attractions, he ended his
hard-sell with, "Remember, Mr. Brown,
this is an investment for the future."
"Listen, young man,"
said Mr. Brown wearily,
"at my time of life I don't even buy
green bananas."

JENNY DE SOUZA

A women walked up to a little old man rocking in a chair on his porch. "I couldn't help noticing how happy you look," she said. "What's your secret for a long, happy life?"
"I smoke three packets of cigarettes a day," he said. "I also drink a case of whiskey a week, eat fatty foods, and never exercise."
"That's amazing," the woman said. "How old are you?"
"Twenty six," he said.

JOE CLARO

To me,
old age is always
fifteen years older
than I am.

BERNARD M. BARUCH

It's ill-becoming
for an old broad to sing about
how bad she wants it.
But occasionally we do.

LENA HORNE

Old age doesn't
stop men from chasing
women – it's just they
can't remember why.

JENNY DE SOUZA

The only ones who don't notice
when your hair starts graying,
your face is sagging,
and your waistline is disappearing
are grandchildren
and the family dog.

GRANDMA JAN

"Now I've reached my sixties I'm going
to apply for a home help," said Charley.
"What?" I replied. "You mean you want
someone to clean and cook for you?"
"No," Charley said,
"I want someone to help me home
from the pub at night."

MIKE KNOWLES

Oldies like to think of themselves
as curmudgeons. Only a misguided
few are incessantly cheerful,
and those people must be avoided
at all costs. Don't criticize them,
just realise they can't help it.
Being disillusioned with the modern
world is our favourite hobby –
no, it's our responsibility.

NIELA ELIASON

Regrets are the natural

property of grey hairs.

CHARLES DICKENS

When you are old you
do not have to use your brains so much
because they are a bit rusty.

KAREN EDWARDS

It's William's sixty-fifth birthday
and his best friend James
is organising a surprise birthday party.
James has arranged for a magician
to make a birthday cake
appear out of a hat.
The magician needs to know
one final detail – how to recognise
the birthday boy.
"That's easy," said James,
"he'll be the one sitting
in the corner crying."

STUART & LINDA MACFARLANE

Isn't it ironic that by the time
you reach an age when you could
really use something that promises
to 'diminish' the appearance of lines,
wrinkles and pores,
your failing old eyes prevent you
finding out how to use the stuff?

JAN MOIR

What a wonderful life I've had!
I only wish I'd realised it sooner.

SIDONIE GABRIELLE COLETTE

I am enjoying to the full
that period of reflection
which is the happiest conclusion
to a life of action.

WILLA CATHER

It's hard for me to get used to
these changing times.
I can remember when the air was clean
and sex was dirty.

GEORGE BURNS

As one grows older, one becomes wiser and more foolish.

FRANÇOIS DE LA ROCHEFOUCAULD

There's a reason why forty, fifty, and sixty don't look the way they used to, and it's not because of feminism, or better living through exercise. It's because of hair dye.

NORA EPHRON

I have got old age sorted.
When sent to the supermarket
I came back with a goldfish.
When asked to wash the dishes
I 'accidentally' broke the best crockery
and when told to do the ironing
I burnt my wife's best blouse.
I have now been banned from doing
all household chores.

BRIAN CLYDE

From birth to age eighteen,
a girl needs good parents;
from eighteen to thirty-five
she needs good looks;
from thirty-five to fifty-five
she needs a good personality;
and from fifty-five on
she needs cash.

SOPHIE TUCKER

"You know what they say
about being as old
as you feel?
I think I'm about 328."

BILL STOTT

If she ever admitted to her real age,
her birthday cake
would be a fire hazard.

AUTHOR UNKNOWN

The only people
who really adore being young
are the middle aged.

CHARLOTTE GRAY

I don't know how you feel
about old age,
but in my case I didn't even
see it coming.
It hit me from the rear.

PHYLLIS DILLER

At my age,
there are hills where
none used to be.

PAM BROWN

From the earliest times
the old have rubbed it into
the young that they are wiser
than they, and before
the young had discovered
what nonsense this was
they were too old,
and it profited them to
carry on the imposture.

W. SOMERSET MAUGHAM

Supreme Court Justice Oliver Wendell
Holmes was asked for his ticket
on a train and couldn't find it.
The conductor, recognising him,
said reassuringly, "Never mind, Sir;
I'm sure you have it somewhere."
"Mr. Conductor," replied Holmes,
"the question is not where is my ticket,
but where am I going."

OLIVER WENDELL HOLMES SNR.

One of the first signs
of getting old
is when your head makes dates
your body can't keep.

KEVIN GOLDSTEIN-JACKSON

The older I get,

he faster I was.

When the American comedian George Burns was ninety he went to see his doctor, complaining of a sore knee. The doctor told him, "You must expect such things at your age."
"Why?" asked Burns. "The other knee's fine and it's just the same age."

Actually sixty isn't such a bad old age.
All right, my eyesight's getting a bit weak
and the optician has given me these
new lenses. Powerful? I'll say so.
They could operate the telescope at the
Mount Palomar Observatory.
And my hairline – that's receded so far
back it's reached my neck.
As for my teeth – they keep falling out
every time I brush them. Have you seen
the price of false ones? No thanks!
I reckon mashed potatoes and minced
beef in gravy isn't so bad after all.

And there are lots of exciting things you
can do with rice pudding and semolina.
These days I spend more time sitting
in front of the television because my joints
are beginning to stiffen up. Suddenly
I'm checking out the zimmer frames
in the local mobility shop.
Hey! That's a nice one.
I wonder if they do it
in red? My attention span –
that's down to three minutes and falling.
But there's one good thing.
At least I've got my health.

MIKE KNOWLES

Wisdom doesn't always show up with age. Sometimes age shows up all by itself.

TOM WILSON

I have thousands of opinions still, and as always, I know nothing.

HAROLD BRODKEY

Fred was determined to keep healthy
in his old age, and when he
turned 60 he decided to walk
five kilometres every day.
He has now reached Adelaide.

GEORGE COOTE

It is better to wear out than rust out.

RICHARD CUMBERLAND

I'm having a glorious
old age.
One of my greatest delights
is that I have outlived
most of the opposition.

MAGGIE KUHN

I do not call myself really old yet.
Not till a young woman
offers me her seat in a railway
compartment will that tragedy
really be mine.

EDWARD VERRALL LUCAS

I am just turning forty
and taking my time about it.

HAROLD LLOYD

The older we get, the

As I have aged I have become the ultimate expert on all political matters. So much so that during news and political programmes on the television I have the right to incessantly shout my views at the screen.

STUART & LINDA MACFARLANE

At sixty you swap the forty push-ups
you did every morning
for an extra forty winks of sleep.

BRIAN CLYDE

better we used to be.

JOHN MCENROE

I often take exercise.
Why only yesterday
I had a breakfast in bed.

OSCAR WILDE

Recently I visited my doctor
for my annual check-up.
He asked me if I have any difficulty
bending over.
"Not in the slightest," I replied,
"but getting back up again
is almost impossible!"

STUART & LINDA MACFARLANE

It is possible that a man
could live twice as long
if he didn't spend the first half
of his life acquiring habits
that shorten the other half.

E. C. MCKENZIE

Anyone can get old.
All you have to do
is to live long enough.

GROUCHO MARX

You know you're ancient when you can remember a time when errors were blamed on human beings rather than computers.

NICOLE REUBENS

Age is just a number…
in my case
a disturbingly large number.

STUART MACFARLANE

My friend Nora is the world's biggest optimist. On reaching her sixtieth birthday she said, "How nice! I've just reached the half-way point."

MIKE KNOWLES

Middle age: when you begin to exchange your emotions for symptoms.

IRVIN S. COBB

I smoke cigars because at my age
if I don't have something to hang onto
I might fall down.

GEORGE BURNS

It worries me, I'm getting so
absent-minded. I mean, sometimes
in the middle of a sentence…

AUTHOR UNKNOWN

The best way to help your children
avoid inheritance tax:
Spend all the money before you
pop your clogs.

ROHANN CANDAPPA

At my age,
by the time I find
temptation,
I'm too tired
to give into it.

E. C. MCKENZIE

Middle age
is when it takes
longer to rest
than to get tired.

DR. LAURENCE J. PETER

For an eighty year old
I have superb stamina…
pity I'm only sixty-two.

LINDA GIBSON

Today I made a very bold decision.
I have decided to stop fixating
on the many, many, many things
that I can no longer do.
Instead I will focus
on the positive and concentrate
my energy on the thing
that I can still do brilliantly –
moan!

BRIAN CLYDE

You're past it when… Your "Go-For-It" has "Gone-For-It!"

AUTHOR UNKNOWN

I have been dead for two years, but I don't choose to have it known.

LORD CHESTERFIELD

I was always taught
to respect my elders
and I've now reached the age
when I don't have to
respect anybody.

GEORGE BURNS

The saddest part of birthdays,
there really is no doubt,
is each year I've more candles
and less breath to blow them out.

DONNA EVLETH

Over sixty is when
your beautician,
your hairdresser
and your dentist
all stroke their heads and sigh.

CHARLOTTE GRAY

It's hard to impress
people with the list
of your body's disasters
when you can't
remember the list!

HELEN EXLEY

I have a simple
philosophy.
Fill what's empty.
Empty what's full.
And scratch
where it itches.

ALICE LEE ROOSEVELT LONGWORTH

If you survive long enough,
you're revered –
rather like an old building.

KATHARINE HEPBURN

I know a fella who had one of those hair transplants and it was kind of touching. He bought a comb and asked if it came with instructions!

ROBERT ORBEN

If you worry, you die.
If you don't worry,
you also die.
So why worry?

MIKE HORN

A hair on the head is worth two in the brush.

OLIVER HERFORD

Sixty! Now is the time to make
your mark on the world –
explore the Antarctic or become
an astronaut. Make your mind up
to take on exciting new challenges –
straight after your afternoon nap.

AUTHOR UNKNOWN

I want to die young
at an advanced age.

MAX LERNER

You know you're
getting older when
you order stewed prunes
and the waiter says :
"Excellent choice."

ART LINKLETTER

I wouldn't say my face
was getting more wrinkled,
but the other day
it took a bead of sweat
two hours to reach my chin.

MIKE KNOWLES

When I was young,
the Dead Sea
was still alive.

GEORGE BURNS

…at my time of life
to look to the future
is to take a very short-term
view of things.

EDWARD ENFIELD

Be kind to your kids,
they'll be choosing your nursing home.

AUTHOR UNKNOWN

The trouble with
beauty is that it is
like being born rich
and getting poorer.

JOAN COLLINS

Old people are fond
of giving good advice;
it consoles them
for no longer
being capable of setting
a bad example.

FRANÇOIS DE LA ROCHEFOUCAULD

Old? He gets tired

brushing his teeth.

LEOPOLD FECHTNER

If you resolve to give up
smoking, drinking and loving,
you don't actually live longer,
it just seems longer.

CLEMENT FREUD

Although I just can't take the plunge into bean sprouts or alfalfa, one day I did put a few carrot sticks and celery stalks into a bag and I took a healthful walk in the park. After a while, I sat down on a bench beside an old man, who was both smoking and eating a chocolate bar, two serious violations of a longevity diet.

"Do you mind my asking how old you are?" I said. "Ninety-two," he replied. "Well, if you smoke and eat that stuff, you're gonna die." He took a hard look at my carrots and celery, and then he said, "You're dead already."

BILL COSBY

The day I give in and allow the word
bifocal to enter my vocabulary,
is the day I'll stop dying my roots,
having my teeth capped
and cantilevering my boobs.
It'll be a courageous moment
and fortunately I shall be
too dead to see it.
"Glasses to glasses and bust to bust…"

MAUREEN LIPMAN

If you can't grow old gracefully, do it any way you can.

E. C. MCKENZIE

Fun is like life insurance:
the older you get,
the more it costs.

FRANK MCKINNEY HUBBARD

Now I've reached my sixties,
my hearing has started to go.
It's what the doctors call
a selective deafness.
I can hear some things
and not others. For example,
I can't hear words like,
"Help me with the washing up,"
"Lend me a tenner, Dad"
and "It's your round George."

MIKE KNOWLES

I don't need you
to remind me
of my age,
I have a bladder
to do that for me.

STEPHEN FRY

Sixty is a funny age.
You're too young to retire
and too old to work.

MIKE KNOWLES

Dear Diary:
I ran a marathon today.
I must remember to ask the organisers
of that 10 kilometre race
if they could make the direction signs
bigger next year.

BRIAN CLYDE

My doctor says
that I am normal for my age.
Normal!! I feel so sad
for all the other 'normal'
old gits out there.

MATHILDE FORESTIER

I might repeat to myself,
slowly and soothingly,
a list of quotations
beautiful from minds
profound; if I can
remember any
of the damn things!

DOROTHY PARKER

When you're a baby
you have skin like a peach.
When you get past fifty
your skin still looks like a fruit...
only this time it's a dried prune.

MIKE KNOWLES

Every year we have the grandchildren
round to play Treasure Hunt
in our garden. We had a pretty good
haul this year; three trowels,
two pairs of secateurs and
a set of false teeth.

STUART & LINDA MACFARLANE

Age seldom
arrives smoothly
or quickly.
It's more often
a succession
of jerks.

JEAN RHYS

"Sixty? Amazing,
that's wonderful –
but we were at the same school –
remember?"

BILL STOTT

My special comb –
the one that has served me well
for over forty years
now has no purpose.
It idles in my
dressing table drawer
alongside my hopes
and aspirations.

STUART & LINDA MACFARLANE

Repeat after me...
I'm sixty but I'm not
an old wreck...

BILL STOTT

When I was seventeen,
I couldn't wait to pick up
my driving license –
now I'm over sixty
I can't wait
to pick up my bus pass.

MIKE KNOWLES

"How old are you?"
asked the little boy.
"Very, very old," I replied.
"Fifty?" quizzed the young lad.
"Best think very, very, very, very old,"
I said softly.

LINDA GIBSON

The trouble
with retirement
is that you never
get a day off.

ABE LEMONS

There are three periods
in life: youth, middle age and
"How well you look."

NELSON A. ROCKEFELLER

Chemical Peel:
a hair – (not to say skin –) raising
method of burning the wrinkles off
the face with strong chemicals,
or possibly with a rotating wire brush.
For those who fancy a complexion
like a brick wall.

CHRISTOPHER MATTHEW

I have started playing football
and have joined an over-sixties team.
I thought I played well in my first game
as I scored four goals.
However, the team captain
was not pleased. He told me to
do exactly the same next week but
to score against the opposition.

STUART & LINDA MACFARLANE

It's never too late to have a happy childhood.

BERKELEY BREATHED

When you've reached
a certain age
and think that a face-lift
or a trendy way of dressing
will make you feel
twenty years younger,
remember – nothing can fool
a flight of stairs.

DENIS NORDEN

You know you're getting on
when your bottom hits the settee
before you've even sat down,
and the supermarket cart
rattles less than your dentures.

JON NEWBOLD

"I don't think that I look
my age, sixty, do you, John?"
"Well, no, Sally, not really.
But you used to."

JOHN MYERS

YOU KNOW YOU'RE OVER SIXTY

when you start receiving birthday cards which don't mention your age.

JON NEWBOLD

Look on the brighter side of being bald.
At least you don't have to wash your hair any more.

DARA O'CONNELL

I thoroughly refuse
to throw away the comb
that I've had for thirty years.
I'm not sure if it's
for sentimental reasons
or the naive optimism
that my hair
may make an unexpected
re-appearance once more.

AMANDA BELL

Just like Hercule Poirot
I like to keep my
brain cells active.
Seven or eight times
every day I give
them a challenging
puzzle to solve –
"Where have I put
my dentures now?"

BRIAN CLYDE

My mother
used to say:
The older you get,
the better you get –
unless
you're a banana.

ROSE NYLUND

The years that a woman
subtracts from her age
are not lost:
they are added
to the ages of other women.

DIANE DE POITIERS

Through no fault of my own,
I have become middle-aged.
It's not a character flaw,
it's just something
that happened when I wasn't
paying attention.

NIELA ELIASON

Longevity is one of the more

dubious rewards of virtue.

NGAIO MARSH

I have found that the moment
I work out how to use
a piece of technology
all its functions will be
automatically updated.

STUART & LINDA MACFARLANE

Sixty is
…when comfort triumphs
at last over fashion.
…when you need to have a rest
after tying your shoelaces.
…when keeping your hair on
means wearing a toupée.

PAM BROWN

People think of growing old
like a disease you catch
when you get to about sixty.

EAMONN BRENNAN

I get up every morning
and dust off my wits,
go pick up the paper and read
the 'obits'.
If my name isn't there
I know I'm not dead;
I get a good breakfast
and go back to bed.

AUTHOR UNKNOWN

Retirement at sixty-five
is ridiculous.
When I was sixty-five
I still had pimples.

GEORGE BURNS

Old people shouldn't
eat health foods.
They need all
the preservatives
they can get.

ROBERT ORBEN

"You know you're over the hill
when your most-loved films
are shown at 11 o'clock
in the morning..."

BILL STOTT

I said to my friend,
"I seem to be losing my sense of taste,
these toffees are inedible!"
That's when she suggested
I remove the wrappers.

STUART & LINDA MACFARLANE

By the time a man
finds greener pastures,
he's too old
to climb the fence.

E. C. MCKENZIE

The older you get
the louder your
snoring becomes.
Fortunately your spouse's
hearing deteriorates
at the same rate.

STUART & LINDA MACFARLANE

Today I took my grandson to the zoo.
As we walked around looking at
the animals he made comments
about how fashionable I looked
in my trendy jeans.
To be honest I thought he was
making fun of me – it wasn't until
later that I realised that in my haste
I'd put on my old decorating trousers –
they have tears and holes all over them.
Fashion? Nonsense!

BRIAN CLYDE

I don't feel old, just downright worn out.

WILL SMITH

"My neighbor has arrived
at the age where,
if he drops $10 in
the collection plate,
it's not a contribution –
it's an investment."

ROBERT ORBEN

I love gardening but, with my
multitude of ailments,
I can't do nearly as much as I used to.
Now my philosophy is, if a weed grows
don't kill it – enjoy it.

STUART & LINDA MACFARLANE

One of the nice things about
old age is that you can whistle
while you brush your teeth.

E. C. MCKENZIE

You know you're over sixty
when you don't bother buying
an answerphone because
you're always in.

JON NEWBOLD

Don't complain
about growing old –
many people don't
have that privilege.

EARL WARREN

Yesterday I found a grey hair.
Yippeeee –
for years my wife
has called me 'baldy'.
There will be no more of that!

STUART & LINDA MACFARLANE

I went to the optician and said,
"My eyesight is getting really bad."
"Sure is," came the reply,
"I'm your husband."

AMANDA BELL

You know you're
over sixty
when you start
wearing silly hats.

JON NEWBOLD

The really frightening
thing about middle age
is the knowledge
that you'll grow out of it.

DORIS DAY

You know you're getting old
when you stoop
to tie your shoes and wonder
what else you can do
while you're down there.

GEORGE BURNS

Take a calcium pill every day.
I got this from a friend who went on
a pre-retirement course costing
(thousands), paid for by somebody else.
"What have you learned?" I asked
when he came back.
"I have learned that everyone over sixty
should take a calcium pill every day."
"Anything else?"
"No."
Bearing in mind the cost of the course,
in passing on this nugget to Oldie readers
I reckon that for once at least this column
is giving value for money.

EDWARD ENFIELD

Live your life and

Young men want to be faithful
and are not,
old men want to be faithless
and cannot.

OSCAR WILDE

When you're sixty
you start bragging
about your age.
How else are you
going to get your
senior discounts?

MELANIE WHITE

forget your age.

NORMAN VINCENT PEALE

I must be getting old...
People are beginning
to tell me I look so young.

LUCY MAUD MONTGOMERY

Life:
your brand new
spectacles are never
as good as
the tatty old pair
they replaced.

STUART McLEAN

If you haven't grown up
by the time you're sixty,
you don't have to.

AUTHOR UNKNOWN

I said to my husband,
my boobs
have gone,
my stomach's gone,
say something nice
about my legs.
He said,
"Blue goes
with everything."

JOAN RIVERS

The secret of staying young
is to live honestly, eat slowly,
and lie about your age.

LUCILLE BALL

Who said you're sixty?
You are just a 20 year old
with 40 years of experience.

AUTHOR UNKNOWN

Sixty! When I was nine

thought twelve was old.

BILL STOTT

Did you ever meet
any Romans, Grandma?

PAULETTE CARON

When you reach sixty
your beautician sends
you this letter.
It says, "Dear Customer,
I can no longer help you.
From this day on
you're on your own."

MICHELE KOLFF

I have joined a gym
and now have my own personal
fitness coach. I am concentrating
on weight training to help improve
my muscles and bones.
He has started me lifting balloons
and hopes that I can progress
to tennis balls soon.

LINDA GIBSON

On mornings such as this
I must remember
that the world is not
upside down – I have
merely fallen out of bed.

STUART & LINDA MACFARLANE

Why don't we have
a bath together,
like we used to?
I don't mind
helping you in and out...

BILL STOTT

I had my front door key
sewn into my underwear
so I didn't lose it.
But in the end
that didn't work either.

HELEN THOMSON

I was born old
and get younger
every day.
At present I am
sixty years young.

HERBERT BEERBOHM TREE

YOU KNOW
YOU'RE OVER SIXTY
...when you really think
that you can predict
the weather by the feeling
in your shin bones.

JON NEWBOLD

You have arrived at old age
when all you can put
your teeth into is a glass.

E. C. MCKENZIE

And you thought
the cellulite of middle age
was hard to face!

ROHANN CANDAPPA

"Yes, yes, you have a good body
for a man of sixty,
but you're only here
to have your bunions treated..."

BILL STOTT

The past is the only dead thing
that smells sweet.

CYRIL CONNOLLY

When you get
to my age,
life seems little more
than one long
march to and from
the lavatory.

JOHN MORTIMER

It's a slow progression –
the more you age the more things
begin to hurt. First it may be
your knees, then your hands,
your hips will follow,
soon afterwards it's your eyes.
Then, one morning, you wake up
and realise that your knees
don't hurt anymore
and your hands are less painful.
That's when you really need
to start worrying.

STUART & LINDA MACFARLANE

Old? He is at the age when all phone numbers in his little black book are doctors.

LEOPOLD FECHTNER

Blepharoplasty:
The operation that takes away the bags under your eyes, the better to allow them to open in stunned belief at the subsequent bill.

CHRISTOPHER MATTHEW

Two fraternity brothers
were attending their class reunion,
the first time they'd seen one another
for thirty years.
One asked, "Is your wife still as pretty
as she was when we were all in
school together?"
"Yeah, she is…
but it takes her an hour longer."

JOHN MYERS

It's funny how
we never get too old
to learn some new ways
to be foolish.

E. C. MCKENZIE

Ienjoy being able
to make a great nuisance
of myself.
I would never swap
that for youth.

HELEN THOMSON

Wow! The 1950's!
Were there dinosaurs then, Grandma?

PAULETTE CARON

My idea of hell is

Experience
is a great advantage.
The problem is
that when you get it,
you're too damned old
to do anything about it.

JIMMY CONNORS

to be young again.

MARGE PIERCY

"Sex after sixty:
When relighting your fire
means paying
the overdue gas bill."

JON NEWBOLD

When you're my age,
you go out to the beach and turn
a wonderful colour. Blue.
It's from holding in your stomach.

ROBERT ORBEN

Her birthday cake
had so many candles on it
she was fined for air pollution.

E. C. MCKENZIE

"I wonder
what you'd
look like
without
your chins?"
"Hmmm."

BILL STOTT

One starts to get young
at the age of sixty,
and then it is too late.

PABLO PICASSO

I used to be indecisive, but now
I'm not so sure.

BOSCOE PERTWEE

Lola's husband Joseph, a merchant,
was asked why he subscribed
to Playboy magazine.
"I read Playboy for the same reason
that I read National Geographic,
so's I can see all the sights
I'm too danged old to visit."

JOHN MYERS

A lifetime of experience
has taught me that
there is no household
appliance that
can't be fixed if you use
a large enough hammer.

BRIAN CLYDE

There are three ways
to tell if you're getting on:
people of your own age start
looking older than you;
you become convinced you're
suddenly equipped with a
snooze button; and you start
getting symptoms in the places
you used to get urges.

DENIS NORDEN

You've got to be fifty-nine
to believe
a fellow is at his best at sixty.

FRANK MCKINNEY HUBBARD

Being sixty brings
out certain advantages.
For example, from now on
your birthday cake
is going to get bigger and bigger
as they try to fit
all those candles on.

MIKE KNOWLES

Dear Diary:
I seem to have gotten into
the habit of repeating
everything twice.
I seem to have gotten into
the habit of repeating
everything twice.

STUART & LINDA MACFARLANE

I have one of those cars
that you don't need to drive
because it operates using a
what-do-you-call-it...
ah, yes, a husband.

MATHILDE FORESTIER

At my age
I don't care if
my mind starts
to wander –
just as long as it
comes back again.

MIKE KNOWLES

Old age is when it takes you longer to get over a good time than to have it.

E. C. MCKENZIE

You're over sixty when
you don't need to chase
women any more –
you just hook them
with your walking stick.

MIKE KNOWLES

I didn't realise when I had my heart attack that it would be the start of a game of one-upmanship. I have four stents so that beats all my friends. One tried to gain an advantage by claiming that his two were the biggest. However, we are now all trumped by anyone with a pacemaker!

STUART & LINDA MACFARLANE

There is no fool like an old fool – you can't beat experience.

JACOB M BRAUDE

I have reached the point where
it is no longer appropriate for me
to say, "I got such a fright
I had a heart attack."
Whenever I do this my partner
dashes for the phone to call
emergency services.

STUART & LINDA MACFARLANE

I'm at an age
where my back goes out
more than I do.

PHYLLIS DILLER

It's not all doom and gloom.
Along with the wrinkles,
hair-loss and clicking knees,
your sixtieth birthday does bring
some undeniable advantages:
1. You can cunningly pretend not to hear
anything you don't want to hear.
2. You can enjoy the cheek
of telling the grandchildren not to do
what you did.
3. Your extra chin can act as a book rest.

JON NEWBOLD

My wife said to me,
"I don't look fifty,
do I Darling?"
I said "Not any more."

BOB MONKHOUSE

My son bought me
one of those new-fangled
GPS watches for my birthday –
not a lot of use to me,
I am still trying to get
the hang of the sundial.

STUART & LINDA MACFARLANE

A couple in their sixties
are on their second honeymoon,
reminiscing about the good old days
when they were newlyweds.
Full of nostalgia, the wife says,
"Do you recall how you used to
nibble on my ear lobes?"
"Yes," replied her husband.
"Well. Why don't you do it anymore?"
"Because by the time
I've put my teeth in,
the urge has gone!"

JENNY DE SOUZA

For every baby born, two women
turn into grandmas.
As a new grandma, you will look in
the mirror and think, "I'm too young
to be a grandma."
But you have to face reality.
You are old enough to be a grandma if…
When you raise your arm to wave,
the flab underneath waves first.
You decide to find a job
and discover the references
on your last resume are all deceased.

MARY MCBRIDGE

The best part of being an oldie is that you get to be eccentric and young people have to be polite and patronize your idiosyncrasies.

NIELA ELIASON

You know you're over sixty
when you can't bear listening
to music louder than one decibel.

MIKE KNOWLES

Despite his age my husband,
bless him,
will still have a go at fixing anything
around the house that goes faulty.
Despite my age I'll still have
a go at finding an expert to sort out
every one of his disasters.

STUART & LINDA MACFARLANE